Vivekananda
Speaks to You

Sri Ramakrishna Math
Mylapore, Chennai - 600 004

Published by
Adhyaksha
Sri Ramakrishna Math
Mylapore, Chennai-4

XXI-16M 1C-9-2010
ISBN 81-7120-999-8

Printed in India at
Sri Ramakrishna Math Printing Press
Mylapore, Chennai-4

PREFACE

Romain Rolland, the great European savant, is a biographer of Swami Vivekananda. About the force and power of the Swami's words, he has said:

I cannot touch these sayings of his, scattered as they are through the pages

of books.... without receiving a thrill

through my body like an electric shock. And what shocks, what transports, must have been produced when in burning words they issued from the lips of the hero!

In this booklet can be discerned the fire of Vivekananda's life-giving message. The reader cannot but be thrilled by the directness of the Swami's appeal, be aroused and energized by the earnestness of his call and the ardour of his message. And, in due course, he will certainly be drawn to a study of the epic life of the Swami and his enlightening and invigorating teachings. There can be no happier experience to the reader than this getting into the Vivekananda domain; for whether his aim is individual betterment, or social amelioration or national service or international integration, or spiritual unfoldment, the safe guide for him is Swami Vivekananda.

The youths are restless today. Though they have a leaning towards glorious ends, they feel frustrated because of lack of dependable guidance. But they can, however, find an unfailing Saviour in Vivekananda. He is physically no more; but that mass of discrimination and wisdom, that Himalayan intellect, that puissant Soul bathed in blessedness, that incarnate Spirit of India, is imperishable. Vivekananda lives in his words, whose living power can be felt as one listens to them.

We beckon India's students to a drink at the Man-making Fountain that Swami

Vivekananda is. His message is a tonic to drooping souls, and he is an Awakener par excellence.

The teachings in this booklet have been selected from various works of the Swami and are presented here in a united form. They originally appeared in the *Vedanta Kesari,* the monthly organ of the Sri Ramakrishna Math, Madras, and are now published as a booklet, so that they may reach a wider circle.

It has been said that if you want to know India, you must read Vivekananda. An Indian birth is a boon indeed. But it has to be followed up by an entry into the halls of India's culture. The first door to this entry is here in these pages. Open and go in.

—Publisher

CONTENTS

Vivekananda Speaks to You

ARISE! AWAKE!

YOUNG men, my hope is in you. Will you respond to the call of your nation? Each one of you has a glorious future if you dare believe me. Have a tremendous faith in yourselves, like the faith I had when I was a child. Have that faith, each one of you in yourself—that eternal power is lodged in every soul—and you will revive the whole of India. Ay, we will then go to every country under the sun, and our ideas will before long be a component of the many forces that are working to make up every nation in the world. We must enter into the life of every race in India and abroad; we shall have to *work* to bring this about. Now for that, I want young men. 'It is the young, the strong, and healthy, of sharp intellect, that will reach the Lord', say the Vedas. This is the time to decide your future-while you possess the energy of youth, not when you are worn out and jaded,

1

but in the freshness and vigour of youth. Work; this is the time, for, the freshest, the untouched and unsmelt flowers alone are to be laid at the feet of the Lord, and such He receives. Rouse yourselves, therefore, for life is short. There are greater works to be done than aspiring to become lawyers and picking quarrels and such things. A far greater work is this sacrifice of yourselves for the benefit of your race, for the welfare of humanity. What is in this life? You are Hindus, and here is the instinctive belief in you that life is eternal. Sometimes I have young men come and talk to me about atheism: *I* do not believe a Hindu can become an atheist. He may read European books, and persuade himself he is a materialist, but it is only for a time. It is not in your blood. You cannot believe what is not in your constitution; it would be a hopeless task for you. Do not attempt that sort of thing. I once attempted it when I was a boy, but it could not be. Life is short, but the soul is immortal and eternal and one thing being certain, death, let us therefore take up a great ideal, and give our whole life to it. Let this be our determination and may He, the Lord, who 'comes again and again for the salvation of His own people', to quote from our scriptures, may the great Krishna bless us, and lead us all to the fulfilment of our aims.

Young men, arise, awake, for the time is propitious. Be bold and fear not. It is only in our scriptures that this adjective is given unto the Lord—*Abhih, Abhih*. We have to become *Abhih,* fearless, and our task will be done. Arise, awake, for your country needs this tremendous sacrifice. It is the young men that will do it. 'The young, the energetic, the strong, the well-built, the intellectual'—for them is the task. And we have hundreds and thousands of such young men. Arise and awake, the world is calling upon you. Arise with enthusiasm in your blood. Think not that you are poor, that you have no friends. Ay, whoever saw money make the man? It is man that always makes the money. The whole world has been made by the energy of man, by the power of enthusiasm, by the power of faith.

NATIONAL EDUCATION

THIS national ship, my countrymen, my friends, my children—this national ship has been ferrying millions and millions of souls across the waters of life. For scores of shining centuries it has been plying across this water, and through its agency, millions of souls have been taken to the other shore, to blessedness. But today, perhaps through your own fault, this boat has become a little damaged, has sprung a leak; and would you therefore curse it? Is it fit that you stand up and pronounce malediction upon it, one that has done more work than any other thing in the world? If there are holes in this national ship, this society of ours, we are its children. Let us go and stop the holes. Let us gladly do it with our hearts' blood; and if we cannot, then let us die. We will make a plug of our brains and put them into the ship, but condemn it never.

Say not one harsh word against this society. I love it for its past greatness. I love you all, because you are the children of gods, and because you are the children of the glorious forefathers. How then can I curse you? Never. All blessings be upon you! I have come to you, my children, to tell you all my plans. If you hear them, I am ready to work with you. But if you will not listen to them, and even kick me out of India, I will come back and tell that we are all sinking! I have come now to sit in your midst and, if we are to sink, let us all sink together, but never let curses rise to our lips.

We must have a hold on the spiritual and secular education of the nation. Do you understand that? You must dream it, you must talk it, you must think it, and you must work it out. Till then there is no salvation for the race. The education that you are getting now has some good points, but it has a tremendous disadvantage which is so great that the good things are all weighed down. In the first place, it is not a man-making education; it is merely and entirely a negative education. A negative education or any training that is based on negation is worse than death. The child is taken to school, and the first thing he learns is, that his father is a fool, the second thing, that his grandfather is a lunatic, the third thing, that all his teachers are hypocrites, the fourth that all the sacred books are lies! By the time he is-sixteen, he is a mass of negation, lifeless and boneless..... Education is not that amount of information that is put into your brain and runs riot there undigested, all your life. We must have life-building, man-making, character-making, assimilation of ideas. If you have assimilated five ideas and made them your life and character, you have more education than any man who has got by heart a whole library. If education is identical with information, the libraries are the greatest sages in the world, and encyclopedias are the Rishis. The ideal, therefore, is that we must have the whole education of our country, spiritual and secular, in our own hands, and it must be on national lines, through national methods as far as practical.

MATTER INTO SPIRIT

WHEN the Aryans reached India they found the climate so hot that they could not work incessantly, so they began to think; thus they became introspective and developed religion. They discovered that there was no limit to the power of the mind; they therefore sought to master that; and through it they learned that there was something infinite coiled up in the frame we call man, which was seeking to become kinetic. To evolve this became their chief aim. Another branch of the Aryans went into the smaller and more picturesque country of Greece, where the climate and natural conditions were more favourable, so their activity turned outward and they developed the external arts and outward liberty. The Greek sought political liberty. The Hindu has always sought spiritual liberty. Both are one-sided. The Indian cares not enough for national protection or patriotism, he will defend only his religion; while with the Greek and in Europe (where the Greek civilisation finds its continuation) the country comes first. To care only for spiritual liberty and not for social liberty is a defect, but the opposite is a still greater defect. Liberty of both soul and body is to be striven for.

Try to be pure and unselfish—that is the whole of religion.

My children, the secret of religion lies not in theories but in practice. To be good and to do good—that is the whole of religion. 'Not he that crieth "Lord," "Lord", but he that doeth the will of the Father.' You are a nice band of young men, and I hope in no distant future many of you will be ornaments of the society and blessings to the country you are born in.

Don't be ruffled if now and then you get a brush from the world; it will be over in no time, and everything will be all right.

Be moral. Be brave. Be a heart-whole man —strictly moral, brave unto desperation.

Don't bother your head with religious theories. Cowards only sin, brave men never, no, not even in mind. Try to love anybody and everybody. Be a *man* and try to make those immediately under your care brave, moral and sympathising. No religion for you, my children, but morality and bravery. No cowardice, no sin, no crime, no weakness—the rest will come of itself. . . . . And don't. . . . . visit a theatre or any enervating entertainment whatever.

We, as a nation, have lost our individuality, and that is the cause of all mischief in India. We have to give back to the nation its lost individuality and raise the masses. The Hindu, the Mohammedan, the Christian, all have trampled them under foot. Again the force to raise them must come from inside, that is, from the orthodox Hindus. In every country the evils exist not with, but against, religion. Religion, therefore is not to blame, but men. To effect this the first thing we need is men, and the next is funds.

Now, good dreams, good thoughts for you. You are good and noble. Instead of materialising the spirit, that is, dragging the spiritual to the material plane, convert the matter into spirit, catch a glimpse at least, every day, of that world of infinite beauty and peace and purity—the spiritual, and try to live in it day and night. Seek not, touch not with your toes even, anything that is uncanny.

SRADDHA

TAKE my advice. Set yourselves wholly to the service of others when you come from your colleges. Believe me, far greater happiness would then be yours, than if you had had a whole treasury full of money and other valuables at your command. . . . Leave aside your thoughts of poverty! In what respect are you poor? Do you feel regret because you have not a coach and pair, or a retinue of servants at your beck and call? What of that? You little know how you can have nothing undone in life, if you labour day and night for others with your heart's blood!

You see, in my travels throughout India all these years, I have come across many a great soul, many a heart overflowing with loving kindness, sitting at whose feet I used to feel a mighty current of strength coursing into my heart, and the words I speak to you are only through the force of that current gained by coming in contact with them!

We want Sraddha, we want faith in our own selves. Strength is life, weakness is death. It is by losing this idea of *Sraddha* that the country has gone to ruin. . . . . So *make men* first. Men we want, and how can men be made unless the *Sraddha* is there?. . . . . We want that education by which character is formed, strength of mind is increased, the intellect is expanded, and by which one can stand on one's own feet.

Haven't you read the stories from the Upanishads? I will tell you one. Satyakama went to live the life of a Brahmacharin with his Guru. The Guru gave into his charge some cows and sent him away to the forest with them. Many months passed by, and when Satyakama saw that the number of cows was doubled, he thought of returning to his Guru. On his way back, one of the bulls, the fire and some animals gave him instruction about the Highest Brahman. When the disciple came back, the Guru at once saw by a mere glance at his face that the disciple had learnt the knowlege of the Supreme Brahman. Now the moral this story is meant to teach is that true education is gained by constant living in communion with Nature.

One should live from one's very boyhood with one whose character is like a blazing fire, and should have before one a living example of the highest teaching. Every boy should be trained to practise absolute *Brahmacharya,* and then only, faith and *Sraddha* will come. In our country the imparting of knowledge has always been through men of renunciation. . . . . We must compile some books with short stories from the Ramayana, the Mahabharata and the Upanishads, etc., in very easy and simple language, and these are to be given to our little boys to read.

Power and things like that will come by themselves. Put yourself to work and you will find such tremendous power coming to you that you will feel it hard to bear it. Even the least work done for others awakens the power within, gradually instils into the heart the strength of a lion. I love you all ever so much, but I would wish you all to die working for others—I should be rather glad to see you do that!

GOOD, BETTER, BEST

Go all of you, wherever there is an outbreak of plague or famine, or wherever the people are in distress, and mitigate their sufferings. At the most you may die in the attempt, what of that? How many like you are taking birth and dying like worms, every day? What difference does that make to the world at large? Die you must, but have a great ideal to die for, and it is better to die with a great ideal in life. On you lie the future hopes of our country. I feel extreme pain to see you leading a life of inaction. Set yourselves to work—to work! Do not tarry—

the time of death is approaching day by day. Do not sit idle, thinking that everything will be done in time later!—Mind—nothing will be done that way.

This life is short, the vanities of the world are transient, but they alone live who live for others, the rest are more dead than alive.

Do any deserve liberty who are not ready to give it to others? Let us calmly and in a manly fashion go to work, instead of dissipating our energy in unnecessary frettings and fumings. I for one thoroughly believe that no power in the universe can withold from anyone anything he really deserves. The past was great no doubt, but I sincerely believe that the future will be more glorious still. May Sankara keep us steady in purity, patience and perseverance!

Ninety per cent of human brutes you see are dead, are ghosts-for none lives, my boys, but he who loves. Feel, my children, feel; feel for the poor, the ignorant, the down trodden, feel till the heart stops and the brain reels and you think you will go mad—then pour the soul out at the feet of the Lord and then will come power, help and indomitable energy....Be not afraid, my children. Look not up in that attitude of fear towards that infinite starry vault as if it would crush you. Wait!—In a few hours more the whole of it will be under your feet. Wait money does not pay, nor name; fame does not pay, nor learning. It is love that pays; it is character that cleaves its way through adamantine walls of difficulties.

Have fire and spread all over. Work, work. Be the servant while leading, be unselfish, and *never listen to one friend in private accusing another*. Have infinite patience, and success is yours. Do not try to 'boss', others. Work, work, for to work only for the good of others is life.

Take care!—Beware of everything that is untrue; stick to truth and we shall succeed, may be slowly, but surely. Work as if on each of you depended the whole work. Fifty centuries are looking on you, the future of India depends on you. Work on. Blessings to you all!

We have not done *badly* in the past; certainly not. Our society is not *bad* but good, only I want it to be better still. Not from error to truth, not from bad to good but from truth to higher truth, from good to better, best. I tell my countrymen that so far they have done well—now is the time to do better.

This is my method—to show the Hindus that they have to give up nothing, but only to move on in the line laid down by the sages, and shake off all inertia, the result of servitude. We must move forward along our own line, our own road. Each nation has a main current in life; in India it is religion. Make it strong, and the waters on either side must move along with it.

Be proud that thou art an Indian, and proudly proclaim 'I am an Indian, every Indian is my brother.' Proudly proclaim at the top of thy voice, 'The Indian is my brother, the Indian is my life, India's gods and goddesses are my God, India's society is the cradle of my infancy, the pleasure-garden of my youth, the sacred heaven, the Varanasi of my old age.' Say, brother, 'The soil of India is my highest heaven, the good of India is my good,' and repeat and pray day and night, 'O Thou Lord of Gauri, O Thou Mother of the Universe, vouchsafe manliness unto me! O Thou Mother of strength, take away my weakness, take away my unmanliness, and—Make me a Man!'

EPIC CHARACTERS

BE not weak, either physically, mentally, morally or spiritually. Rama and Sita are the ideals of the nation. All children, especially girls, worship Sita. The height of a woman's ambition is to be like Sita, the pure, the devoted, the all-suffering. When you study these characters, you can at once find the devoted, the all-suffering. When you study these characters, you can at once find out how different is the ideal in India from that of the West. For the race, Sita stands as the ideal of suffering. The West says, 'Do! Show your power by doing.' India says 'Show your power by suffering.' The West has solved the problem of how much a man can have; India has solved the problem of how little a man can have. Sita is typical of India, the idealized India. There is no other Pauranika story that has so permeated the whole nation, so entered into its very life, and has so tingled in every drop of blood of the race as this ideal of Sita. Sita is the name in India for everything that is good, pure and holy; everything that in woman we call womanly.

In speaking of the Mahabharata, it is simply impossible to present the unending array of the grand and majestic characters of the mighty heroes depicted by the genius and mastermind of Vyasa. The internal conflicts between righteousness and filial affection in the mind of the God-fearing, yet feeble, old, blind king Dhritarashtra, the majestic character of the grandsire Bhishma, the noble and virtuous nature of the royal Yudhishthira, and of the other four brothers as mighty in valour as in devotion and loyalty, the peerless character of Krishna unsurpassed in human wisdom, and not less brilliant, the characters of the women—the stately queen Gandhari, the loving mother Kunti, the ever-devoted and all-suffering Draupadi—these and hundreds of other characters of the Epic and those of the Ramayana have been the cherished heritage of the whole Hindu world for the last several thousands of years and form the basis of their thoughts and of their moral and ethical ideas. In fact the Ramayana and the Mahabharata are the two encyclopaedias of the ancient Aryan life and wisdom, portraying an ideal civilization, which humanity has yet to aspire after.

Sacrifices, genuflexions, mumblings and mutterings are not religion. They are only good if they stimulate us to the brave performance of beautiful and heroic deeds, and lift our thoughts to the apprehension of the divine perfection. What good is it, if we acknowledge in our prayers that God is the Father of us all, and in our daily lives do not treat every man as our brother?

What about religion? Has it to remain or vanish? If it remains, it requires its experts, its soldiers. The monk is the religious expert, having made religion his one metier of life. He is the soldier of God. What religion dies, so long as it has a band of devoted monks?

This is the theme of Indian lifework, the burden of her eternal songs, the backbone of her existence, the foundation of her being, the *raison d'etre* of her very existence—the spiritualization of the human race.

And I challenge anybody to show one single period of her national life when India, was lacking in spiritual giants, capable of moving the world. Her work is spiritual. Her influence has always fallen, upon the world like that of the gentle dew, unheard and scarcely marked, yet bringing into bloom the fairest flowers of the earth.

One vision I see clear as life before me—
that the ancient Mother has awakened once
more, sitting on Her throne, rejuvenated,
more glorious than ever. Proclaim Her to
all the world with the voice of peace and
benediction.

TAPASYA

IN the world take always the position of
the giver; help, give service, give any little
thing you can, but *keep out barter*. Make
no conditions and none will be imposed.
Let us give out of our own bounty, just as
God gives to us.

Look at the 'Ocean' and not at the 'wave.'
Get the mercy of God and of His greatest
children; these are the two chief ways to
God. The company of these children of light
is very hard to get; five minutes in their
company will change a whole life, and if you
really want it enough, one will come to you.

Our best work is done, our greatest
influence is exerted when we are without
thought of self.

Today God is being abandoned by the world, because He does not seem to be doing enough for the world. So they say, 'Of what good is He?' Shall we look upon God as a mere municipal authority?

True, power comes of austerities; but again working for the sake of others itself constitutes *Tapasya* (practice of austerity). The Karma Yogins regard work itself as a part of *Tapasya*. As on the one hand the practice of *Tapasya* intensifies altruistic feelings in the devotee and actuates him to unselfish work, as also the pursuit of work for the sake of others carries the worker to the last function of *Tapasya* namely the purification of the heart, and lead him thus to the realization of the Supreme Atman. . . . In fact disinterested work is quite as difficult as *Tapasya*.

First you have to build the body by good nutritious food—then only will the mind be strong. The mind is but the subtle part of the body. You must retain great strength in your mind and words. *I am low, I am low*—repeating these ideas in the mind, man belittles and degrades himself. He alone who is always awake to the idea of freedom becomes free; he who thinks he is bound endures life after life in the state of bondage. Be a hero. Always say, *have no fear.* Fear is death, fear is sin, fear is hell, fear is unrighteousness, fear is wrong life. All the negative thoughts and ideas that are in this world have proceeded from this evil spirit of fear. Therefore I say *Be fearless, be fearless.*

Well, you consider a man as educated if only he can pass some examinations and deliver good lectures. The education which does not help the common mass of people to equip themselves for the struggle for life, which does not bring out strength of character a spirit of philanthropy and the courage of a lion—is it worth the name? Real education is that which enables one to stand on one's own legs. The education that you are receiving now in schools and colleges is only making you a race of dyspeptics. You are working like machines merely, and living a jelly-fish existence.

You are thinking yourselves highly educated. What nonsense have you learnt? Getting by heart the thoughts of others in a foreign language and stuffing your brain with them and taking some university degrees you consider yourselves educated! Fie upon you! Is this education? What is the goal of your education? Either a clerkship, or being a scheming lawyer or at the most a Deputy Magistracy, which is another form of clerkship—isn't that all? What good will it do to you or the country at large?.... Throw aside your scriptures in the Ganges and teach the people first the means of procuring their food and clothing, and then you will find time to read to them the scriptures. If their material wants are not removed by the rousing of intense activity, none will listen to words of spirituality.

You must learn to make the physique very strong, and teach the same to others. Don't you find me exercising everyday with dumb-bells even now? Walk in the mornings and evenings, and do physical labour. Body and mind must run parallel.

My hope of the future lies in the youths of character—intelligent, renouncing all for the service of others and obedient—who can sacrifice their lives in working out my ideas and thereby do good to themselves and the country at large. . . . If I get ten or twelve boys with the faith of Nachiketa, I can turn the thoughts and pursuits of this country in a new channel.

SOUND THE DAMARU

YOU have now to make the character of Mahavira your ideal. See how at the command of Ramachandra crossed the ocean. He had no care for life or death! He was a perfect master of his senses and wonderfully sagacious. You have now to build your life on this great ideal of personal service. Through that all the other ideals will gradually manifest in life. Obedience to the Guru without questioning, and strict observance of Brahmacharya—this is the secret of success.

Are not drums made in the country? Are not trumpets and kettledrums available in India? Make the boys hear the deep-toned sound of these instruments. Hearing from boyhood the sound of effeminate forms of music the country is wellnigh converted into a country of women. What more degradation can you expect? The Damaru and horn have to be sounded; drums are to be beaten so as to raise the deep and martial notes... The music which awakens only the softer feeling of man is to be stopped now for some time. The people are to be accustomed to hear the Dhrupad music. Through the thunder roll of the dignified Vedic hymns, life is to be brought back into the country. In everything the austere spirit of heroic manhood is to be revived. . . . In eating, dressing or lying, in singing or playing, in enjoyment or disease, always manifest the highest moral courage.

If you think any work difficult, then do not come here. Through the grace of God all paths become easy. Your work is to serve the poor and miserable. Without distinction of caste or colour, and you have no need to think of the results. Your duty is to go on working, and then everything will follow of itself. My method of work is to construct and not pull down. After so much austerity I have understood this as real truth. God is present in every Jiva; there is no other God besides that. Who serves Jiva serves God indeed.

'Comfort' is no test of truth; on the contrary truth is often far from being comfortable. If one intends to really find truth, one must not cling to comfort. . . . Sacrifice is necessary.

Do not 'pity' anyone. Look upon all as your equals, cleanse yourself of the primal sin of inequality. We are all equal, and must not think, 'I am good and you are bad, and I am trying to reclaim you.'

Thought is all important, for 'what we think we become'.

The eternal law is self-sacrifice, not self assertion.

Although we appear as little waves, the whole sea is at our back and we are one with it. No wave can exist of itself.

The ideal woman in India is the mother, the mother first and the mother last. The word *woman* calls up to the mind of the Hindu, motherhood; and God is called Mother. . . To the ordinary man in India the whole force of womanhood is concentrated in motherhood... The ideal of womanhood in India is motherhood—that marvellous, unselfish, all suffering, ever-forgiving mother.

The Indian race never stood for wealth. Although they acquired immense wealth, perhaps more than any other nation ever acquired, yet the nation did not stand for wealth. It was a powerful race for ages, yet we find that that nation never stood for power, never went out of the country to conquer. Quite content within their own boundaries, they never fought anybody. The Indian nation never stood for imperial glory. Wealth and power, then, were not the ideals of the race. What then? That nation, among all the children of men, has believed and believed intensely, that this life is not real. The real is God; and they must cling unto that God, through thick and thin. Religion came first. The Hindu man drinks religiously, sleeps religiously, walks religiously, marries religiously, robs religiously. The vitality of the race, the mission of the race is religion; and because that has not been touched, that race lives. The Indian nation never will be a powerful, conquering people—never. They will never be a great political power; that is not their business, that is not the note India has to play in the great harmony of nations. But what has she to play? God, and God alone.

BUDDHA AND JESUS

THE bond between the teacher and the taught—that is peculiar to India. The teacher is not a man who comes just to teach me and I pay him so much and there it ends. In India it is really like an adoption. The teacher is more than my own father and I am truly his child, his son in every respect. I owe him obedience and reverence first, before my own father even; because, they say, the father gave me this body, but he showed me the way to salvation, he is greater than father. And we carry this love, this respect for our teacher all our lives.

Monks go from door to door, so that religion is brought to everybody without charge, except perhaps a broken piece of bread (given away to the monk as alms). That is why you see the lowest of the low in India holding the most exalted religious ideas. It is all through the work of these monks.

Take the Sermon on the Mount and the Gita—they are simplicity itself. Even the street-walker can understand them. How grand! In them you find the truth clearly and simply revealed.

Buddha preached the most tremendous truths. He taught the very gist of the philosophy of the Vedas to one and all without distinction, he taught it to the world at large, because one of his great messages was the equality of man. Men are all equal.

No concession there to anybody! Buddha was the great preacher of equality. Every man and woman has the same right to attain spirituality—that was his teaching. The difference between the priests and the other castes, he abolished. Even the lowest were entitled to the highest attainments; he opened the door of Nirvana to one and all.

The life of Buddha has an especial appeal. All my life I have been very fond of Buddha but not of his doctrine. I have more veneration for that character than for any other. That boldness, that fearlessness and that tremendous love! He was born for the good of men. How to help them,—that was his only concern. Throughout his life he never had a thought for himself... And consider his marvellous brain! No emotionalism. That giant brain never was superstitious.

Six hundred years before the birth of Christ, at the time when Buddha lived, the people of India must have had wonderful education. Extremely free-minded they must have been. Great masses followed him.

Kings gave up their thrones; queens gave up their thrones. People were able to appreciate and embrace his teaching, so revolutionary, so different from what they had been taught by the priests through the ages. But their minds must have been unusually free and broad.

If Buddha was great in life, he was also great in death... Even when dying he would not claim any distinction for himself. I worship him for that.

It is not easy to be a disciple; great preparations are necessary; many conditions have to be fulfilled.

Vedanta formulates, not universal brotherhood, but universal oneness.

The history of the world is the history of persons like Buddha and Jesus.

The older I grow the more everything seems to me to lie in manliness. This is my new gospel.

I am the servant of the servants of the servants of Buddha. Who was there ever like him—the Lord—who never performed one action for himself—with a heart that embraced the whole world! So full of pity that he—prince and monk-would give his life to save a little goat!

You cannot begin too early to teach the highest spiritual truths.

Read the Gita and other good works on Vedanta.

The present system of education is all wrong. The mind is crammed with facts before it knows how to think. Control of the mind should be taught first. If I had my education to get over again and had my voice in the matter, I would learn to master my mind first, and then gather facts if I wanted them. It takes people a long time to learn things because they cannot concentrate their minds at all.

From dreams awake, from bonds be free. Be not afraid.

THE ROAD TO THE GOOD

APPRECIATION or no appreciation, I am born to organise these young men; nay, hundreds more in every city are ready to join me, and I want to send them rolling like irresistible waves over India bringing comfort, morality, religion, education to the doors of the meanest and the most down-trodden. And this I will do or die.

Three men cannot act in concert together in India for five minutes. Each one struggles for power and in the long run the whole organization comes to grief. Lord! Lord! When will we learn not to be jealous!

Why was it so easy for the English to conquer India? It was because they are a nation, we are not. When one of our great men dies, we must sit for centuries to have another—they can produce them as fast as they die. The difficulty is the dearth of great ones. Why so? Because they have such a bigger field of recruiting their great ones, we have so small. A nation of 300 millions has the smallest field of recruiting its great ones compared with nations of thirty, forty or sixty millions, because the number of educated men and women in those nations is so great. This is the greatest defect in our nation and must be removed. Educate and raise the masses, and thus alone a nation is possible.

I have come to this conclusion that there is only one country in the world which understands religion—it is India; that with all their faults the Hindus are head and shoulders above all other nations in morality and spirituality and that with proper care and attempt and struggle of all disinterested sons, by combining some of the active and heroic elements of the West with the calm virtues of the Hindus there will come a type of men far superior to any that have ever been in this world.

Europe has always been the source of social and Asia of spiritual power; and the whole history of the world is the tale of the varying combinations of those two powers.

Multitude counts for nothing. A few heart-whole, sincere, and energetic men can do more in a year than a mob in a century.

Let me tell you a little personal experience. When my Master left the body, we were a dozen penniless and unknown young men. Against us were a hundred powerful organizations, struggling hard to nip us in the bud. But Ramakrishna had given us one great gift—the desire and the life-long struggle not to talk alone, but to *live the life*.. And today all India knows and reverences the Master, and the truths he taught are spreading like wild fire. Ten years ago, I could not get a hundred persons together to celebrate his birthday anniversary. Last year (1894) there were fifty thousand

Neither numbers, nor powers, nor wealth, nor learning, nor eloquence, nor anything else will prevail but *purity,* living *the life,* in one word, *anubhuti,* realization.

Let there be a dozen such lion-souls in each country, lions who have broken their own bonds, who have touched the Infinite, whose whole soul is gone to Brahman, who care neither for wealth nor power, nor fame, and these will be *enough* to shake the world.

Don't look back—forward! Infinite energy, infinite enthusiasm; infinite daring and infinite patience—then alone can great deeds be accomplished.

If it is the Lord's work, the right man for the right place will be forthcoming in the right time.

Great work requires great and persistent effort for a long time. Neither need we trouble ourselves if a few fall. It is the nature of things that many should fall that troubles should come, that tremendous difficulties should arise, that selfishness and all the other devils in the human heart should struggle hard, when they are about to be driven out by the fire of spirituality. The road to God is the roughest and steepest in the universe. It is a wonder that so many succeed, no wonder that so many fall. Character has to be established through a thousand stumbles.

The history of civilization is the progressive reading of spirit into matter.

Too much sentiment hurts work. 'Hard as steel and soft as a flower' is the motto.

Without regular exercise the body does not keep fit; talking, talking all the time brings illness—know this for certain.

The best work is only done by alternate repose and work.

We Indians suffer from a great defect, viz., we cannot make a permanent organization—and the reason is that we never like to share power with others and never think of what will come after we are gone.

I fervently wish no misery ever came near any one, yet it is that alone that gives us an insight into the depths of our lives, does it not? In our moments of anguish, gates barred for ever seem to open and let in many a flood of light.

Really there is no greater sin than cowardice; cowards are never saved—that is sure. I can stand everything else, but not that. If one gets one blow, one must return ten with redoubled fury,. then only one is a man.. the coward is an object to be pitied.

I want to see you die even, but you must make a fight. Die in obeying commands like a soldier, and go to Nirvana, but no cowardice.

We may read books, hear lectures and talk miles, but experience is the one teacher, the one eye-opener. It is best as it is. We learn, through smiles and tears we learn.

In this world of Maya one need not injure but 'spread the hood without striking'. That is enough.

The Sun	— Knowledge
The stormy water	— Work
The lotus	— Love
The serpent	— Yoga
The swan	— The Self
The Motto	— May the Swan

(the Supreme Self) send us that

The snake represents mysticism; the sun knowledge; the worked up waters activity; the lotus love; the swan the soul in the midst of all.

GOD'S POEM

ONE of the greatest lessons I have learned in my life is to pay as much attention to the means of work as to its end. All the secret of success is there: to pay as much attention to the means as to the end.

The weak have no place here, in this life or in any other life. Weakness leads to slavery. Weakness leads to all kinds of misery physical and mental. Weakness is death.

This is the great fact: strength is life; weakness is death. Strength is felicity, life eternal, immortal.

Therefore I say, we require super-divine power. Super-human power is not strong enough. Super-divine strength is the only way, the one way out.

We only get what we deserve.

Man is an infinite circle whose circumference is nowhere, but the centre is located on one spot, and God is an infinite circle whose circumference is nowhere, but whose centre is everywhere.

A man can be of gigantic intellect, yet spiritually he may be a baby.

Religion is not in doctrines, in dogmas, not in intellectual argumentation, it is being and becoming; it is realization.

The wicked see this world as a perfect hell, and the good as a perfect heaven. Lovers see this world as full of love, and haters as full of hatred. Fighters see nothing but strife, and the peaceful nothing but peace. The perfect man sees nothing but God.

Of all the forces that have worked and are still working to mould the destinies of the human race, none, certainly, is more potent than that the manifestation of which we call religion.

The exact definition of the Sanskrit word Rishi is a seer of Mantras—of the thoughts conveyed in the Vedic hymns.

Man is man, so long as he is struggling to rise above Nature, and this Nature is both internal and external.

The mainspring of the strength of every race lies in its spirituality and the death of that race begins the day that spirituality wanes and materialism gains ground.

Truth does not pay homage to any society, ancient or modern. Society has to pay homage to Truth, or die.

In Buddha we had the great, universal heart, and infinite patience making religion practical and bringing it to everyone's door. In Sankaracharya we saw tremendous intellectual power throwing the scorching light of reason upon everything. We want today that bright sun of intellectuality joined with the heart of Buddha, the wonderful infinite heart of love and mercy. This union will give us the highest philosophy. Science and religion will meet and shake hands. Poetry and philosophy will become friends. This will be the religion of the future, and if we can work it out, we may be sure that it will be for all times and peoples.

Who enjoys the picture, the seller or the seer? The seller is busy with his accounts, computing what his gain will be, how much profit he will realize on the picture. His brain is full of that. He is looking at the hammer and watching the bids. He is intent on hearing how fast the bids are rising. That man is enjoying the picture, who has gone there without any intention of buying or selling. He looks at the picture and enjoys it.

I never read of any more beautiful conception of God than the following: 'He is the Great Poet, the Ancient Poet; the whole universe is His Poem, coming in verses and rhymes and rhythms, written in infinite bliss.'

I have been asked many times, 'Why do you use that old word, God?' Because it is the best word for our purpose; you cannot find a better word than that, because all the hopes, aspirations and happiness of humanity have been centred in that word. It is impossible now to change the word.

Man according to the Vedanta philosophy is the greatest being that is in the universe, and this world of work the best place in it, because only herein is the greatest and the best chance for him to become perfect. Angels or gods, whatever you may call them, have all to become men, if they want to become perfect. This is the great centre, the wonderful opportunity—this human life.

The doctrine which stands out luminously in every page of the Gita is intense activity, but in the midst of it, eternal calmness.

The Vadanta teaches men to have faith in themselves first. The Vedanta says, a man who does not believe in himself is an atheist. Not believing in the glory of our own soul is what the Vedanta calls atheism. . . It recognizes no sin, it only recognizes error; and the greatest error, says the Vedanta, is to say that you are weak, that you are a sinner, a miserable creature, and that you have no power, and you cannot do this and that.

If faith in ourselves had been more extensively taught and practised, I am sure a very large portion of the evils and miseries that we have would have vanished. Throughout the history of mankind, if any motive power has been more potent than another in the lives of all great men and women, it is that of faith in themselves.

The old religions said that he was an atheist who did not believe in God. The new religion says that he is the atheist who does not believe in himself.

Feel like Christ and you will be a Christ; feel like Buddha and you will be a Buddha.

I accept all religions that were in the past and worship with them all; I worship God with everyone of them in whatever form they worship Him. I shall go to the mosque of the Mohammedan; I shall enter

the Christian's church and kneel before
the crucifix; I shall enter the Buddhistic
temple, where I shall take refuge in
Buddha and in his law. I shall go into the
forest and sit down in meditation with the
Hindu, who is trying to see the light which
enlightens the heart of everyone. Not only
shall I do all these, but I shall keep my
heart open for all that may come in the
future. Is God's book finished? Or is it
still a continuous revelation, going on? It
is a marvellous book—these spiritual
revelations of the world. The Bible, the
Vedas, the Koran and all other sacred books
are but so many pages, and an infinite
number of pages remain yet to be unfolded.

What is my plan? In the first place I
would ask mankind to recognize this
maxim—'Do not destroy'. Iconoclastic
reformers do no good to the world. Break
not, pull not anything down, but build Help,
if you can; if you cannot, fold your hands
and stand by and see things go on. Do not
injure, if you cannot render help. Say not a
word against any man's convictions so far

as they are sincere. Secondly, take man where he stands and from there give him a lift.

Do you think you can teach even a child? You cannot. The child teaches himself. Your duty is to afford opportunities and to remove obstacles.

WORK LIKE A MASTER

ART Science and Religion are but three different ways of expressing a single truth. But in order to understand this, we must have the theory of Advaita.

From the high spiritual flights of the Vedanta philosophy, of which the latest discoveries of science seem like echoes, to the low ideas of idolatry with its multifarious mythology, the agnosticism of the Buddhists and the atheism of the Jains, each and all have a place in the Hindu's religion.

By the Vedas no books are meant. They mean the accumulated treasury of spiritual laws discovered by different persons in different times. The discoverers of these laws are called Rishis and we honour them as perfected beings. Some of the very greatest of them were women.

Creation is without beginning or end. There never was a time when there was no creation. Creation and Creator are two lines without beginning and without end, running parallel to each other.

You are the Children of God, the sharers of immortal bliss, holy and perfect beings. Ye divinities on earth—sinners! It is a sin to call a man so; it is a standing libel on human nature. You are souls immortal, spirits free, blest and eternal; ye are not matter, ye are not bodies; matter is your servant, not you the servant of matter.

A man ought to live in this world like a lotus leaf, which grows in water but is never moistened by water; so a man ought to live in the world—his heart to God and his hands to work. Reaching God, seeing God, becoming perfect even as the Father in Heaven is perfect, constitutes the religion of the Hindus.

Man is to become divine by realizing the divine. Idols or temples or churches or books are only the supports, the helps, of his spiritual childhood, but on and on he must progress.

I am not a Buddhist, as you have heard, and yet I am. If China or Japan or Ceylon follows the teachings of the great Master, India worships him as God incarnate on earth. Shakya Muni came not to destroy, but he was the fulfilment, the logical conclusion, the logical development of the religion of the Hindus.

In religion there is no caste; caste is simply a social institution.

When a man has reached the highest, when he sees neither man nor woman, neither sex, nor creed, nor colour, nor birth, nor any of these differentiations, but goes beyond and finds that divinity which is the real man behind every human being—then alone he has reached the universal brotherhood, and that man alone is a Vedantist.

Each soul is potentially divine.

The goal is to manifest this divine within, by controlling nature, external and internal.

Do this either by work, or worship, or psychic control, or philosophy, by one or more, or all of these—and be free.

This is the whole of religion. Doctrines, or dogmas, or rituals, or books, or temples, or forms are but secondary details.

Help and not Fight.

Assimilation and not Destruction.

Harmony and Peace and not Dissention.

These, then—the Shastras, the Guru, and the Motherland—are the three notes that mingle themselves to form the music of the works of Vivekananda. . . . . These are the three lights burning within that single lamp which India by his hand lighted and set up for the guidance of her own children and the world. . . . .

—Sister Nivedita